CULTURE IN ACTION

Exploring Other Worlds

WHAT IS SCIENCE FICTION?

Claire Throp

Chicago, Illinois

www.heinemannraintree.com
Visit our website to find out more information about Heinemann-Raintree books.

To order:

☎ Phone 888-454-2279

🖥 Visit www.heinemannraintree.com to browse our catalog and order online.

Edited by Louise Galpine and Diyan Leake
Designed by Victoria Allen
Original illustrations © Capstone Global Library Ltd 2011
Illustrated by Randy Schirz
Picture research by Hannah Taylor

Originated by Capstone Global Library Ltd
Printed in and bound in China by CTPS

14 13 12 11 10
10 9 8 7 6 5 4 3 2 1

Library of Congress Cataloging-in-Publication Data
Throp, Claire.
  Exploring other worlds : what is science fiction? / Claire Throp.
    p. cm. -- (Culture in action)
  Includes bibliographical references and index.
  ISBN 978-1-4109-3928-9
  1. Science fiction--History and criticism--Juvenile literature.
  2. Science fiction films--History and criticism--Juvenile literature. I. Title.
  PN3433.5.T57 2010
  809.3'8762--dc22
                                    2009052814

Acknowledgments
The author and publishers are grateful to the following for permission to reproduce copyright material:Alamy Images pp. **8** (© Mary Evans Picture Library), **12** (© Pictorial Press Ltd), **15** (© RIA Novosti), **19** (© Pictorial Press Ltd), **21** (© Lebrecht Music & Arts), **27** (© Picture Contact); Corbis pp. **10** (John Springer Collection), **17** (Sunset Boulevard); Getty Images pp. **6** (Time Life Pictures/Mansell), **14** (Roger Viollet/Boyer), **26** (WireImage/Ferdaus Shamim); The Kobal Collection p. **20** (Lucas Film/20th Century Fox); Lebrecht Music & Arts p. **7** (RA); NASA pp. **4** (Charles Pete Conrad), **16**; Rex Features pp. **5** (© BuenaVist/Everett), **11** (Olycom SPA), **18**, **22** (© Paramount/Everett), **23** (Everett Collection), **24** (James Fraser).

Cover photograph of a science fiction magazine cover reproduced with permission of Corbis (Forrest J. Ackerman Collection).

We would like to thank Brooks Peck and Jackie Murphy for their invaluable help in the preparation of this book.

Every effort has been made to contact copyright holders of any material reproduced in this book. Any omissions will be rectified in subsequent printings if notice is given to the publisher.

Disclaimer
All the Internet addresses (URLs) given in this book were valid at the time of going to press. However, due to the dynamic nature of the Internet, some addresses may have changed, or sites may have changed or ceased to exist since publication. While the author and publisher regret any inconvenience this may cause readers, no responsibility for any such changes can be accepted by either the author or the publisher.

Author
Claire Throp is an experienced editor and author of books for young people.

Literacy consultant
Jackie Murphy is Director of Arts at the Center of Teaching and Learning, Northeastern Illinois University. She works with teachers, artists, and school leaders internationally.

Expert
Brooks Peck is a curator at the Science Fiction Museum and Hall of Fame in Seattle, as well as an author and screenwriter.

Contents

Some words are printed in bold, **like this**. You can find out
what they mean by looking in the glossary on page 30.

What Is Science Fiction?

Have you ever imagined what it would be like to travel back in time? You may have wondered whether aliens exist or what it would be like to go to Mars. Science fiction is the name given to a type of story in which the writers imagine just that sort of thing. Science fiction stories often include time travel, space travel, and scientific experiments. They may involve robots or aliens. Science fiction often tries to imagine what things will be like in the future.

Certain **themes** (ideas) run through science fiction stories. They have changed over time as **technology** and science have developed. People's ideas about the world around them have also had an effect on what type of science fiction is most popular at the time. This book gives you an introduction to the world of science fiction.

While fantasy stories are about impossible things, science fiction looks at what is possible. Space travel has always been a popular theme in science fiction.

Robots with personalities are common in science fiction. The movie *Wall.E*, about a robot who was designed to clean up all the waste on Earth, was released in 2008.

Science fiction or fantasy?

Very often, science fiction and fantasy are on the same shelves in a library or bookstore. The difference is that science fiction is based more on scientific fact, whereas fantasy is totally made up. Science fiction stories are often set in a world that is different from our own, but in scientific terms it would be possible for that world to exist.

Why is it called science fiction?

The term "science fiction" was first used by a U.S. magazine editor, Hugo Gernsback. Gernsback had started the magazine *Amazing Stories* in 1926. He planned to include fiction (stories) that would help to teach young readers about science. Originally, the term he came up with was "scientifiction." He changed it to "science fiction" three years later.

Wars Between Worlds

One of the most popular **themes** of science fiction is alien invasion. In the late 1800s, many invasion books were written. Most were based on invasions by other countries. When the first alien invasion stories appeared, they were linked with **colonialism**. Colonialism is when one country takes over the running of another country. For example, in the 1800s, Great Britain was powerful and took over many other countries.

Alien invasion

In 1898 the British author H. G. Wells wrote a book called *The War of the Worlds*. In it, Britain is invaded by technologically **superior** aliens from Mars. Wells wanted the British to see what it was like to be colonized by more advanced beings. In the story, it seems at first that the British soldiers will easily beat the invading Martians. However, the **military** is unable to beat the aliens. Eventually, the Martians are defeated by tiny living things called microorganisms rather than by the might of the British.

H. G. Wells wrote many science fiction stories and even **predicted** the **atomic bomb** in a 1914 story.

Wells's book challenged scientific ideas of **evolution**. Evolution was a popular scientific topic of the time. Evolution is the gradual development of living things over millions of years. Wells challenges evolution by having the most simple creatures—the microorganisms—defeat the most advanced creatures.

Martians have invaded!

Science fiction has sometimes had a great effect on people's lives. In 1938 a radio program caused panic across the United States. People tuned in and thought aliens had invaded from Mars! In fact, it was a play based on *The War of the Worlds*. People were confused because it sounded like it was a real news program. The man responsible was the U.S. actor Orson Welles.

Sci-fi stories

A wide range of science fiction was produced in the early years of the 1900s. H. G. Wells wrote many books. Karel Čapek introduced the word "robot" for the first time in his play *R.U.R.* Movies such as *A Trip to the Moon* (1902) and *Metropolis* (1927) were made.

Magazines

The number of magazines publishing science fiction grew rapidly. Short stories did not take long to read, so they could easily be fit into busy lives. Pictures were included that made the stories even more exciting. This was a time when people were recovering from World War I (1914–1918). Science fiction stories were strange and powerful. By reading books and magazines, people could escape from the hardship of their lives. Many science fiction writers had their first stories published in the U.S. magazine *Amazing Stories*.

VALLEY OF INVISIBLE MEN *by* EDMOND HAMILTON

SEE BACK COVER

Amazing STORIES

MARCH
20c

The RAID FROM MARS *by* MILES J. BREUER

AND GREAT STORIES BY
ED EARL REPP
ROBERT BLOCH
F. A. KUMMER, JR.

The magazine *Amazing Stories* ran for nearly 80 years. It was the first magazine to print only science fiction.

Sound effects

Even today, people still make **sound effects** for radio or television. For example, they might use a jar of rice to make the sound of rain or a snake. With a friend, pretend that you have to make sound effects for a play.

Steps to follow:

1. Decide what your play will be about. It could be about a person traveling in a time machine or aliens attacking Earth.

2. Think about the sounds that will be needed. Make a note of all the sounds you will need to tell your story. Be sure you know the order in which the sound effects need to be performed.

3. Figure out what instruments or other items can be used to make those sounds. For example, you could try drums or a triangle.

4. Experiment with the speed of the sounds or how loud they are. The sound of an alien walking toward you could be made by a **rhythmic** sound getting louder and louder.

9

Alien Invasion

In the United States in the 1950s, more science fiction was written than ever before. This was partly a result of the threat of **Communism**. Communism was a **political** system that existed in the **Soviet Union** (what is now Russia and other countries). The idea of Communism was that everyone is equal. In practice, it meant a **dictatorship**, with the country run by one man. The U.S. government was strongly opposed to Communism. The fear of "others," which in the United States at the time usually meant Communists, was the inspiration for many science fiction writers.

Movies in the 1950s

One of the most famous movies of the time was *Invasion of the Body Snatchers* (1956). It was based on a book by the U.S. author Jack Finney.

Reports of flying saucers and an alien spaceship supposedly found in Roswell, New Mexico, in 1947 led to many science fiction movies. *Invasion of the Body Snatchers* was just one of them.

In *Invasion of the Body Snatchers*, alien seed pods fall to Earth and grow into copies of people they come into contact with. In the book, only one man fights against the aliens, and eventually he forces them to leave Earth. In the movie, however, it is left open as to whether the alien takeover can be stopped, as the pods have already spread across the country.

The aliens have no emotion and think alike. This was what many people thought about Communists at the time. Although the author and filmmakers have said that they did not mean the movie to be against Communism, many people may have believed otherwise.

Still popular

Alien invasion movies are still made today. *Monsters vs. Aliens* (2009) is a recent example with a twist. Aliens attack Earth, and the government asks monsters that it has captured to help defend the world from the aliens. Reese Witherspoon (right) provided the voice for one of the characters.

An anti-war movie

The Day the Earth Stood Still (1951) was different from most of the movies made in the 1950s. As much of the United States had strong feelings against Communism, it was a brave movie to make. The alien Klaatu and his robot Gort come to Earth to warn humans that they face destruction unless they stop their violent behavior.

In *The Day the Earth Stood Still*, the message is that nuclear weapons will lead to disaster for the human race.

Friendly aliens

Discovering aliens on Earth is not always a bad thing. In the 1982 movie *E. T.: the Extra-Terrestrial*, an alien gets left behind when his fellow aliens leave Earth. E. T. becomes friends with the boy who finds him. *Lilo and Stitch* (2002) also features an alien that escapes to Earth and becomes friends with Lilo, a young girl.

Draw your own science fiction monster

Do you like watching movies and television shows with monsters in them? See if you can draw your own monster.

Steps to follow:

1. Decide what type of monster you are going to create. It does not have to be scary—it could be a friendly alien or a helpful robot. If you think about the personality of the monster, it will help you to decide what it looks like. Think about where it will live and if it has a name.

2. Sketch your monster. Decide what color it will be, its size, and how many arms it has. Think about why it has these features. Maybe it needs to have reflective skin so that the rays from its sun bounce off it. Maybe it has a tail to help it balance because its head is very big. What can your science fiction monster do?

3. Once you have made your sketches, make a poster of your monster. Try using different materials such as paint, felt-tip pens, and fabrics. Put it up on your bedroom wall. (Don't forget to check with a parent or caregiver that it is okay to do this.)

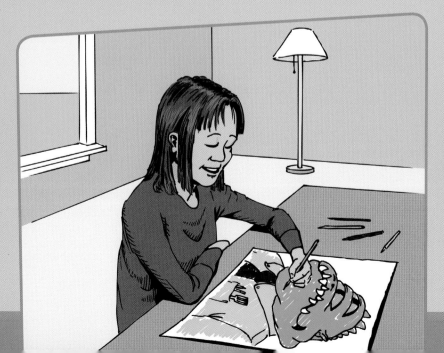

Space Travel

Are you fascinated by space and what might be out there waiting to be discovered? Lots of science fiction writers are. Voyages to the Moon have been particularly popular. The first mention came in a **spoof** story written about 1,850 years ago by a Roman author named Lucian. In the story, the author and his friends sail to the Moon on a waterspout! In *From the Earth to the Moon*, a story written in 1865 by the French author Jules Verne, people were sent into space in a spaceship that was fired from a large cannon.

Jules Verne

Jules Verne is now thought to be "the father of science fiction." He was born in 1828 in Nantes, France. Verne studied law but then became interested in the theater. He began to write plays. He and his wife traveled a lot, often sailing in their own boat. Finally, after years of trying, he had a book published called *Five Weeks in a Balloon*. He went on to write many more science fiction and adventure stories, including *Journey to the Center of the Earth*. Verne died in 1905.

The "space race"

The United States and the **Soviet Union** competed to see who could reach space first. The Soviet Union won the first round when it sent *Sputnik 1* into orbit (a path in space circling the Earth) in October 1957. *Sputnik 1* was a **satellite**, a spacecraft that traveled around Earth to explore space. The following year the United States launched a satellite.

A dog named Laika became the first living being in orbit in space when she went up in *Sputnik 2* in November 1957.

The journey to the Moon that was so often written about finally happened in 1969. As in Jules Verne's story, the astronauts set off from Florida.

Humans in space

In 1961 the Soviet **cosmonaut** Yuri Gagarin became the first person in space. Two years later, Valentina Tereshkova was the first woman in space. The United States hit back in July 1969, when Neil Armstrong became the first person to walk on the Moon. This was something that science fiction writers had been imagining for so many years—and now it had finally happened.

Movies, television shows, and books exploring space became very popular in the 1960s. Television series such as *Star Trek* and *Lost in Space* and the movie *2001: A Space Odyssey* (1968) explored the idea of living in space.

Is science fiction bad?

Not everybody likes space travel stories. The astronaut Buzz Aldrin was one of the first people to walk on the Moon in 1969. He has complained about science fiction because it creates unrealistic ideas. He thinks that these stories make ordinary people believe in amazing things that cannot happen—at least not in the near future. Science fiction makes actual space exploration seem dull in comparison.

Avatar

Avatar (2009) is a movie that explores the continuing fascination with space travel. It is set in the future and is about humans trying to colonize a planet called Alpha Centauri B-4. Avatar became the highest-earning movie of all time, a fact that shows how popular science fiction is.

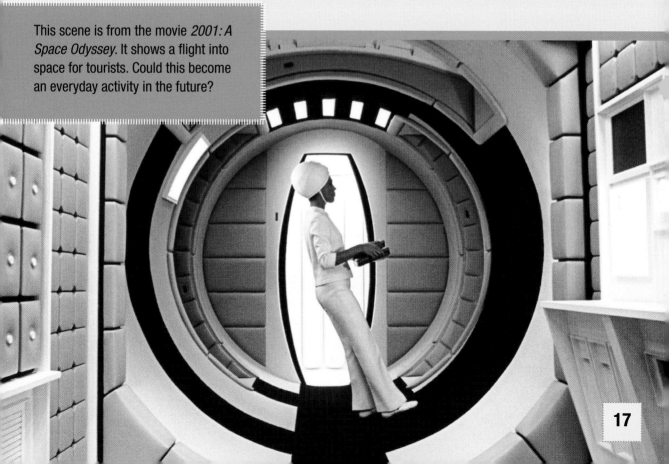

This scene is from the movie *2001: A Space Odyssey*. It shows a flight into space for tourists. Could this become an everyday activity in the future?

Time Travel

Time travel is a **theme** that crops up throughout science fiction history. Who would not be excited by the idea of going back in time to meet a favorite person from history? Or going forward in time to see what the world is like in the future?

Doctor Who first appeared on television in 1963. The Doctor could travel anywhere in any time period, and he did so in a blue **police call box** called the Tardis. The original *Doctor Who* finished in 1989. However, it was brought back in 2005 and now has millions of viewers around the world. There are also other programs linked to *Doctor Who*, including *Torchwood*.

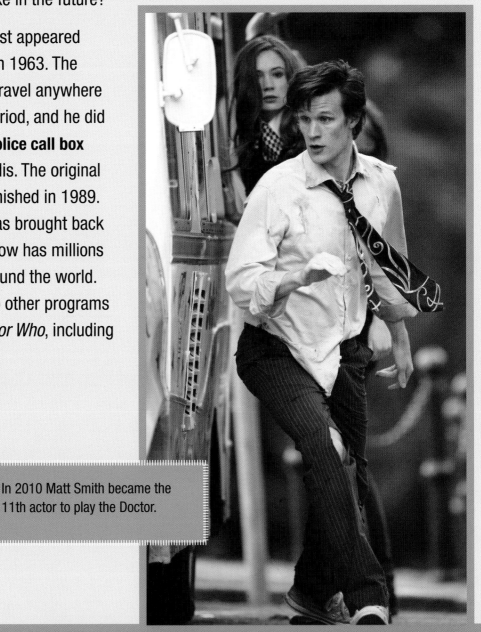

In 2010 Matt Smith became the 11th actor to play the Doctor.

Time-travel movies

In the 1980s several movies were made about time travel. In *Back to the Future* (1985), the main character is sent back in time and meets his parents while they are in high school! This movie looks at how changing events in the past can affect the future.

However, time-travel stories can involve evil as well as good. *The Terminator* (1984) saw a robot from the year 2029 coming back to the present. The robot's aim is to kill a woman before she has a son, because her son will grow up to be the robot's enemy.

The Time Machine

The Time Machine was written by H. G. Wells in 1895. The main character—a scientist—travels forward in time to the year 802,701. By this time, the human race has split into two groups, one strong and one weak. The scientist then travels onward and sees the end of the human race. The book was another response to the fascination with **evolution** and **decadence** that people in Britain had at the time.

Space Opera

The movie *Star Wars* (1977) helped to make science fiction very popular. It is known as a space opera. Space opera focuses on adventures set in space and the people who live there. The first space operas appeared in magazines such as *Amazing Stories* in the late 1920s. At the time, the term "space opera" was used to suggest that it was bad science fiction. However, that changed in the 1970s, when characters became more realistic.

Star Trek is also considered to be a space opera. The original television show was made in the 1960s, but it did not become popular until it was rerun in the 1970s. The show was set in a future where people had overcome **prejudice**, war, and poverty, and worked together to explore the other planets.

The *Star Wars* movies are still popular today.

Women writers

It is often thought that science fiction is mainly written by men for boys and other men. However, from the 1970s, more women began to write science fiction. During the 1970s women continued to fight for equal representation in society with men. Ursula K. Le Guin, author of *The Left Hand of Darkness*, and Joanna Russ, who is famous for writing *The Female Man*, were writing science fiction at this time. Women created more realistic characters than had usually existed in science fiction.

Of course, there had been women writers of science fiction before. Some people believe that *Frankenstein* was the first science fiction book. It was written by Mary Shelley in 1818. She also wrote another science fiction tale called *The Last Man*. This story was set in a future in which disease had wiped out everyone apart from one man.

Mary Shelley wrote about the need for sympathy and cooperation in society as well as the uses of science.

A Step Too Far?

The relationship between humans and **technology** is a science fiction **theme** that became common in the 1980s. This was as a result of an increase in technology in people's daily lives at the time. People have created powerful computers and machines. Science fiction expressed the fear that machines would become more powerful than their human creators and take over the world.

Some science fiction has robots as central characters. *Transformers* was originally a television cartoon in 1984. The fight between two races of robot—the Autobots and the Decepticons—moves to Earth and threatens human life. In 2007 *Transformers* was made into a movie. There are also computer games based on the story.

Transformers continues the theme of good versus evil.

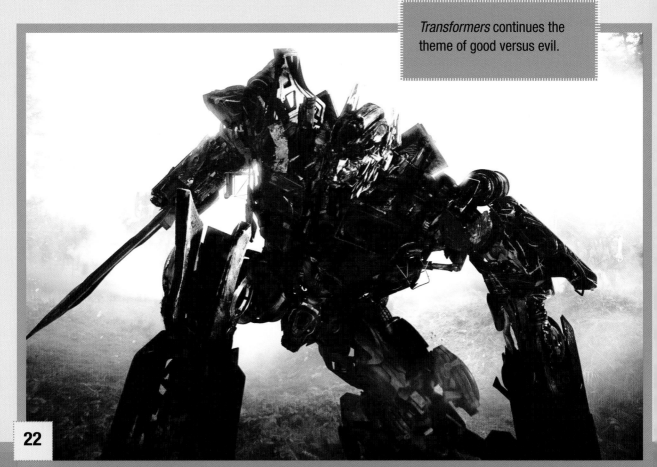

Cyborgs

Cyborgs are beings that have both human parts and mechanical parts. Many science fiction stories have been created about cyborgs. An Australian television series called *Cybergirl* is one example. The main character comes to Earth to meet the humans on whom she was modeled. More famous cyborgs include Darth Vader from *Star Wars* and the Cybermen from *Doctor Who*.

In real life, the first cyborg was a U.S. man named Jesse Sullivan. He lost his arms in an accident, and they were replaced with artificial arms. They are connected to his body in such a way that he can move them almost as he would his real arms.

Metropolis

In 1926 a movie called *Metropolis* was made in Germany. The movie was set around the year 2000. It was about an inventor who creates a female robot. The robot was an evil double of the woman loved by the main character of the movie.

Cloning

Cloning is just one of the science fiction subjects currently attracting attention. When a living thing is **cloned**, it means it is copied exactly. Dolly the sheep is the most famous cloned animal, but there have been others. The idea is not only to provide body parts for humans, but also to stop animals from becoming extinct (dying out).

Scientists worry because people's knowledge of issues such as cloning often comes only from science fiction, which is not always accurate. An example is the movie *Jurassic Park* (1993), in which dinosaurs have been cloned from dinosaur blood found in mosquitoes trapped in a fossil called amber.

The Island (2005) is a movie in which human clones are told that they are being kept away from others to protect them from disease. They are really being kept in case their rich human doubles ever need a new body part.

Dolly the sheep was the first animal to be cloned from adult cells. She was born in 1996.

Interview your favorite character

Have you ever seen interviews on television? An interview is when one person asks another person questions about his or her life. With a friend, pretend to be your favorite science fiction characters and interview each other.

Steps to follow:

1. Choose which character you want to be. Maybe you could be Frankenstein's monster or Ginormica from *Monsters vs. Aliens*.

2. Dress up like the character. For example, if you are Mr. Spock from *Star Trek*, you could make some pointy ears.

3. With your friend, write down some questions you want to ask. It is probably best to each use the same questions.

4. How would your favorite character respond? Make notes on the character so you can figure out what he or she would say, as well as how to move and make your voice sound to seem like your character.

5. Find two chairs and start interviewing. You could even record the interviews and show them to friends.

25

The Future of Science Fiction

For many years, science fiction has been based on scientific fact. Now scientists seem to be using ideas from science fiction to help science. A group of researchers studying infectious diseases (diseases that can spread very easily) used **zombie** movies to help them in their work in fighting disease. This is because they wanted to work with the idea of something that is difficult to kill, the way zombies are!

Science fiction is as popular today as it has ever been. Science fiction movies such as *E. T.*, *Star Wars*, and *Avatar* have earned a lot of money. Science fiction computer games are also among the most popular. In 2007 the Xbox game *Halo 3* sold $170 million worth of copies in one day. This set a record for an entertainment product. Science fiction comics, graphic novels, and books are read by many people. Some people collect science fiction items such as props, autographs, toys, and models. There is certainly no sign that this popularity will fade in the near future.

Science fiction conventions are meetings of science fiction and fantasy fans, many of whom dress up as their favorite characters.

Asimo is an intelligent robot. It can turn on lights and open doors. It can even recognize people and use their name!

Many of the technological advances imagined by science fiction over the years have actually come about. However, **technology** is improving all the time. Science fiction follows scientific change and builds on it. There will always be a chance for writers to imagine something new.

Timeline

1818	Mary Shelley writes *Frankenstein*
1864	Jules Verne writes *Journey to the Center of the Earth*
1895	H. G. Wells writes *The Time Machine*
1898	H. G. Wells writes *The War of the Worlds*
1902	The movie *A Trip to the Moon* is released
1914—1918	World War I
1926	The movie *Metropolis* is released
	Hugo Gernsback starts the magazine *Amazing Stories*
1938	The play *The War of the Worlds* is broadcast on the radio in the United States
1939—1945	World War II
1945	The **atomic bomb** is first used
1951	The movie *The Day the Earth Stood Still* is released
1956	The movie *Invasion of the Body Snatchers* is released
1957	"The Space Age" begins with the Soviet **satellite** *Sputnik 1*
1961	Soviet **cosmonaut** Yuri Gagarin is the first person in space

1963	*Doctor Who* first appears on television in the United Kingdom
	Soviet cosmonaut Valentina Tereshkova becomes the first woman in space
1968	The movie *2001: A Space Odyssey* is released
1969	U.S. astronaut Neil Armstrong becomes the first person to walk on the Moon
1977	The movie *Star Wars* is released
1982	The movie *E. T.: the Extra-Terrestrial* is released
1984	The movie *The Terminator* is released
1985	The movie *Back to the Future* is released
1996	Dolly the sheep is created from **cloned** adult cells
2007	The movie *Transformers* is released
2009	The movie *Monsters vs. Aliens* is released
	The movie *Avatar* is released

Glossary

atomic bomb bomb with massive energy created by the splitting of atoms

clone make an exact physical copy

colonialism when one country takes over the running of another country

Communism political system that existed in the Soviet Union (what is now Russia and other countries) from 1922 to 1991. Goods and property are supposed to be held equally by everyone. In reality, the system usually results in a dictatorship, with the country run by one person.

cosmonaut Russian astronaut; person trained to travel in space

decadence fall of moral and cultural standards in society. For example, people become lazy and greedy.

dictatorship when one person is in charge of a country and rules harshly

evolution gradual development of living things over time

military armed forces such as the army or navy

police call box telephone box that was in a public place for the police to use, or for members of the public to contact the police, before there were two-way radios or cell phones

political relating to how a country is run

predict be able to describe future events before they actually happen

prejudice when people are treated unfairly because of their race, gender, or beliefs

rhythmic happening with a regular beat. Music usually has a rhythmic beat.

satellite spacecraft that travels around Earth to explore space

sound effect noise that is made to sound like something else—for example, thunder. Sound effects are often used in movies and in radio and television programs.

Soviet Union short name for the Union of Soviet Socialist Republics, the country that later broke up into the Russian Federation and other countries

spoof story that is not meant to be serious or realistic

superior better than something or someone else

technology use of tools and power to invent new machines and to make machines work

theme topic or subject. For example, time travel is a theme of science fiction.

zombie person who is brought back from the dead. Zombies often appear in science fiction because they are difficult to stop.

Find Out More

Books

Hamilton, John. *Science Fiction*. Edina, Minn.: ABDO, 2009.

Hamilton, John. *You Write It: Science Fiction*. Edina, Minn.: ABDO, 2009.

Hyland, Tony. *Film and Fiction Robots* (Robots and Robotics series). North Mankato, Minn.: Smart Apple Media, 2008.

Websites

www.sciencenewsforkids.org/articles/SciFiZone.asp
Find out more about science stories on this website.

www.starwars.com/kids/
If you are a fan of *Star Wars*, this is the website to visit!

Index